Roman visits the dentist

Roman was sad, he cried and be bawled. He wanted his mummy, he called and he called.

Mummy told Roman "I know it's hurting you, but It's just your new teeth, there's nothing I can do"

Mummy brushed
Roman's teeth both
morning and night
New ones all came
through it was a
beautiful sight

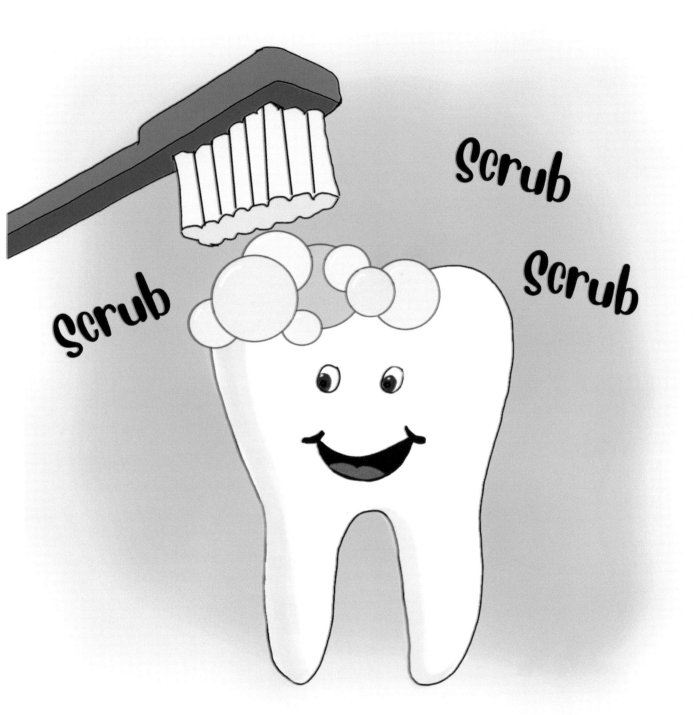

On Wednesday morning he
woke up with a shout.

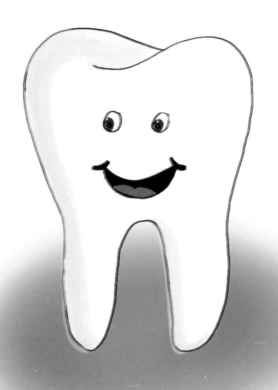

Toby the tooth
was finally out!

Then one sunny morning
he woke with a moan
The pain in old toby was
making him groan

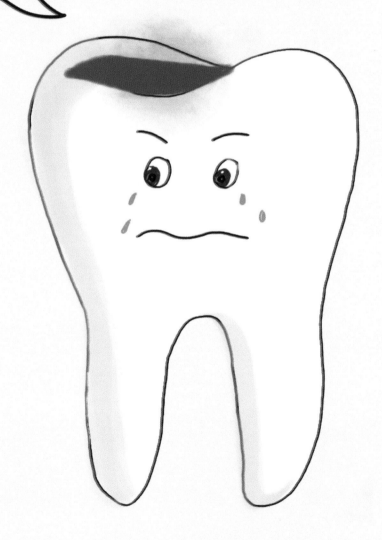

As the years passed by, his teeth all in a row Roman's food choices began to grow and to grow

Ask when you got your teeth, you can even colour them in

Mummy said quick
there's one thing we
can do
Of to the dentist this
afternoon for you

He walked into the room, blue walls and big chair

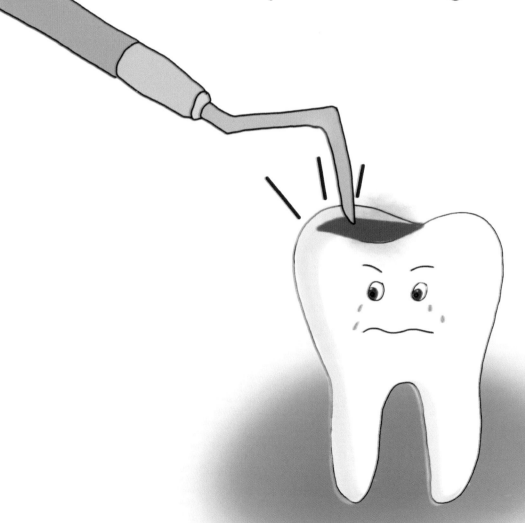

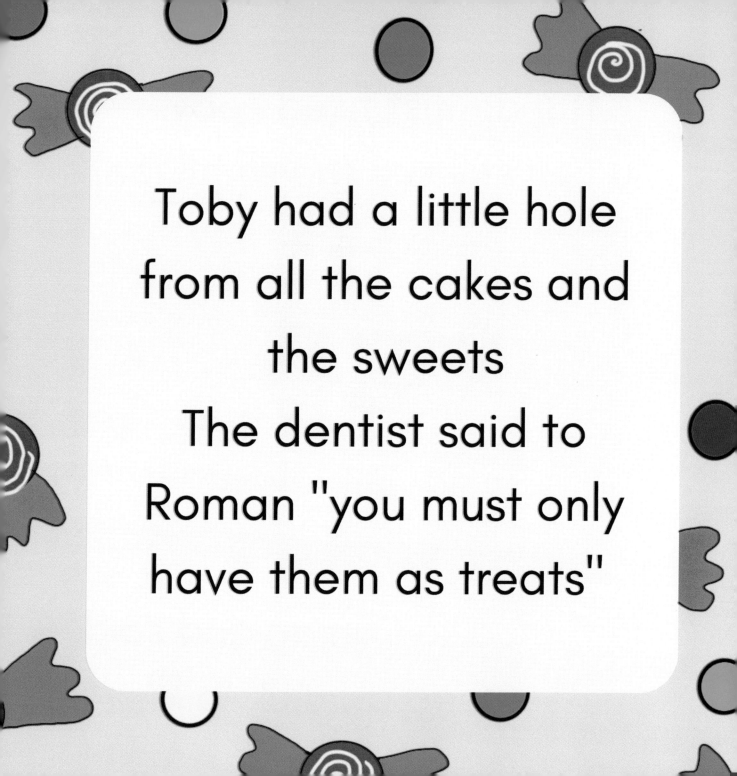

Toby had a little hole from all the cakes and the sweets
The dentist said to Roman "you must only have them as treats"

The dentist fixed Toby,
you can still see the small mark

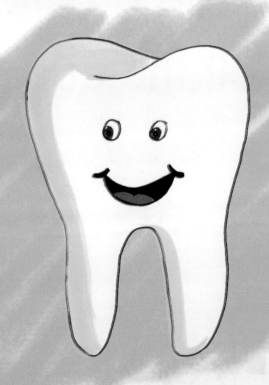

He turned to Roman and said
"We need a quick talk"

"You must take care
of your teeth and
brush twice a day
Now you can go back
home to play"

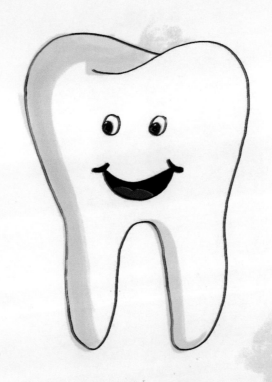

Printed in Great Britain
by Amazon

23379435R00016